In the Community

At the Pharmacy

By Julia Jaske

I see pharmacists
at the pharmacy.

I see medicine at the pharmacy.

4   I see drops at the pharmacy.

I see technicians at the pharmacy. 5

6 I see lotion at the pharmacy.

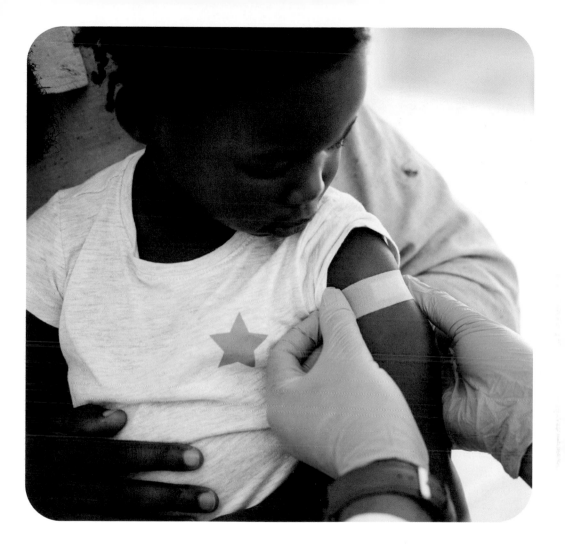

I see bandages at the pharmacy. 7

8 I see customers at the pharmacy.

I see vaccines at the pharmacy.

10 I see gloves at the pharmacy.

I see prescriptions
at the pharmacy.

12 I see computers at the pharmacy.

I see cashiers at the pharmacy.

Word List

pharmacy

pharmacists

medicine

drops

technicians

lotion

bandages

customers

vaccines

gloves

prescriptions

computers

cashiers

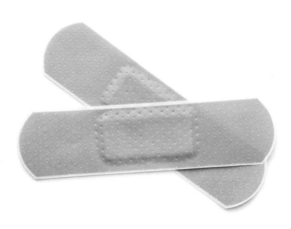

- I see pharmacists at the pharmacy.
- I see medicine at the pharmacy.
- I see drops at the pharmacy.
- I see technicians at the pharmacy.
- I see lotion at the pharmacy.
- I see bandages at the pharmacy.
- I see customers at the pharmacy.
- I see vaccines at the pharmacy.
- I see gloves at the pharmacy.
- I see prescriptions at the pharmacy.
- I see computers at the pharmacy.
- I see cashiers at the pharmacy.

CHERRY BLOSSOM PRESS

Published in the United States of America by Cherry Lake Publishing Group
Ann Arbor, Michigan
www.cherrylakepublishing.com

Book Designer: Keri Riley

Photo Credits: cover: © StratfordProductions/Shutterstock; page 1: © SofikoS/Shutterstock; page 2: © Gorodenkoff/Shutterstock; page 3: © i viewfinder/Shutterstock; page 4: © Alexander Raths/Shutterstock; page 5: © SofikoS/Shutterstock; page 6: © smoxx/Shutterstock; page 7: © PeopleImages.com – Yuri A/Shutterstock; page 8: © Tyler Olson/Shutterstock; page 9: © Tong_stocker/Shutterstock; page 10: © Microgen/Shutterstock; page 11: © Idutko/Shutterstock; page 12: © Zamrznuti tonovi/Shutterstock; page 13: © LEDOMSTOCK/Shutterstock; page 14: © Anton Starikov/Shutterstock

Note from publisher: Websites change regularly, and their future contents are outside of our control. Supervise children when conducting any recommended online searches for extended learning opportunities.

Cherry Blossom Press is an imprint of Cherry Lake Publishing Group.

Library of Congress Cataloging-in-Publication Data

Names: Jaske, Julia, author.
Title: At the pharmacy / written by Julia Jaske.
Description: Ann Arbor, Michigan : Cherry Blossom Press, 2023. | Series: In the community | Audience: Grades K-1 | Summary: "At the Pharmacy explores the sights and sounds of the pharmacy. It covers people and objects found at the pharmacy. Uses the Whole Language approach to literacy, combining sight words and repetition to build recognition and confidence. Simple text makes reading these books easy and fun. Bold, colorful photographs that align directly with the text help readers with comprehension"– Provided by publisher.
Identifiers: LCCN 2023003178 | ISBN 9781668927229 (paperback) | ISBN 9781668929742 (ebook) | ISBN 9781668931226 (pdf)
Subjects: LCSH: Readers (Primary) | LCGFT: Readers (Publications).
Classification: LCC PE1119.2 .J367 2023 | DDC 428.6/2–dc23/eng/20230206
LC record available at https://lccn.loc.gov/2023003178

Printed in the United States of America
Corporate Graphics